50 Savory Premium Pies from Around the World Recipes

By: Kelly Johnson

Table of Contents

- Thai Green Curry Soup
- Vietnamese Pho
- Japanese Ramen
- Mexican Tortilla Soup
- Indian Butter Chicken Soup
- Mediterranean Lentil Soup
- Chinese Hot and Sour Soup
- Moroccan Harira Soup
- Korean Kimchi Stew
- Italian Minestrone
- Caribbean Goat Curry
- Ethiopian Misir Wat
- Greek Avgolemono Soup
- Spanish Gazpacho
- Peruvian Chicken Soup (Aguadito de Pollo)
- Indonesian Soto Ayam
- Lebanese Fattoush Salad Bowl
- French Onion Soup
- Brazilian Feijoada Stew
- Turkish Ezogelin Soup
- Israeli Shakshuka
- Thai Tom Yum Soup
- Mexican Pozole
- Russian Borscht
- Sri Lankan Dhal Curry
- Jamaican Red Bean Soup
- Chinese Wonton Soup
- Indian Sambar
- Cambodian Amok Fish Stew
- Nigerian Egusi Soup
- Egyptian Molokhia
- Italian Pappa al Pomodoro
- Afghan Ashak
- Malaysian Laksa
- Vietnamese Bun Bo Hue

- Filipino Sinigang na Baboy
- Pakistani Haleem
- Tunisian Brik
- Persian Fesenjan
- Greek Beef and Tomato Stew
- South African Bunny Chow
- Japanese Miso Soup
- Filipino Adobo
- Hawaiian Poke Bowl
- South Korean Bibimbap
- Cuban Ropa Vieja
- Israeli Sabich Bowl
- Moroccan Chickpea and Tomato Soup
- New Zealand Kumara Soup
- Indonesian Gado-Gado

Thai Green Curry Soup

Ingredients:

- 2 tablespoons green curry paste
- 1 can (14 oz) coconut milk
- 3 cups vegetable or chicken broth
- 1 cup mushrooms, sliced
- 1/2 cup baby carrots, sliced
- 1/2 cup bell pepper, sliced
- 1/2 cup tofu or chicken, cubed
- 2 tablespoons fish sauce
- 1 tablespoon lime juice
- Fresh basil or cilantro for garnish
- Lime wedges for serving

Instructions:

1. In a large pot, heat the green curry paste over medium heat for 1-2 minutes until fragrant.
2. Add the coconut milk and broth, then bring to a simmer.
3. Add the mushrooms, carrots, bell peppers, and tofu or chicken. Cook for 5-7 minutes until vegetables are tender.
4. Stir in fish sauce and lime juice.
5. Serve hot, garnished with fresh basil or cilantro and lime wedges on the side.

Vietnamese Pho

Ingredients:

- 1 lb beef brisket or flank steak
- 6 cups beef broth
- 1 onion, halved
- 2-inch piece ginger, sliced
- 2 star anise
- 1 cinnamon stick
- 1 tablespoon fish sauce
- 1 teaspoon sugar
- 8 oz rice noodles
- Fresh herbs (cilantro, basil), bean sprouts, lime wedges, and chili for garnish

Instructions:

1. In a large pot, add the beef, beef broth, onion, ginger, star anise, cinnamon stick, fish sauce, and sugar. Bring to a boil, then lower to a simmer for about 1.5-2 hours.
2. While the broth is simmering, cook the rice noodles according to the package directions.
3. Once the broth is ready, strain out the solids and return the broth to the pot.
4. Thinly slice the cooked beef and add it to bowls.
5. Pour the hot broth over the beef and noodles.
6. Garnish with fresh herbs, bean sprouts, lime wedges, and chili. Serve hot.

Japanese Ramen

Ingredients:

- 4 cups chicken or pork broth
- 2 cups water
- 2 tablespoons soy sauce
- 1 tablespoon miso paste
- 1 tablespoon sesame oil
- 2 cloves garlic, minced
- 2 soft-boiled eggs
- 1/2 cup sliced mushrooms
- 1/4 cup green onions, chopped
- 4 oz ramen noodles
- 1/2 cup spinach or bok choy

Instructions:

1. In a pot, combine the broth, water, soy sauce, miso paste, sesame oil, and garlic. Bring to a simmer.
2. Cook the ramen noodles according to the package instructions.
3. Add the mushrooms and spinach or bok choy to the broth and simmer for 3-4 minutes.
4. To serve, divide the noodles into bowls, pour the broth over, and top with a soft-boiled egg, green onions, and additional toppings of choice (like nori or sesame seeds).

Mexican Tortilla Soup

Ingredients:

- 1 tablespoon olive oil
- 1 onion, chopped
- 2 garlic cloves, minced
- 1 can (14 oz) diced tomatoes
- 4 cups chicken broth
- 1 teaspoon cumin
- 1 teaspoon chili powder
- 1/2 teaspoon paprika
- 1 cup cooked chicken, shredded
- 1/4 cup tortilla strips
- 1/4 cup fresh cilantro, chopped
- Lime wedges for garnish
- Avocado, sliced for garnish

Instructions:

1. Heat olive oil in a pot over medium heat. Add onions and garlic and sauté until softened.
2. Stir in diced tomatoes, chicken broth, cumin, chili powder, and paprika. Bring to a boil, then simmer for 10 minutes.
3. Add shredded chicken and tortilla strips, then simmer for an additional 5-7 minutes.
4. Serve hot, garnished with fresh cilantro, lime wedges, and avocado slices.

Indian Butter Chicken Soup

Ingredients:

- 2 tablespoons butter
- 1 onion, chopped
- 2 garlic cloves, minced
- 1 tablespoon grated ginger
- 2 teaspoons garam masala
- 1 teaspoon turmeric
- 1 teaspoon cumin
- 1 can (14 oz) diced tomatoes
- 1/2 cup heavy cream
- 2 cups chicken broth
- 1 lb chicken breast, cubed
- Fresh cilantro for garnish

Instructions:

1. In a pot, melt butter over medium heat. Add onion, garlic, and ginger, cooking until softened.
2. Stir in garam masala, turmeric, and cumin, cooking for 1-2 minutes.
3. Add diced tomatoes, heavy cream, and chicken broth. Bring to a simmer.
4. Add chicken and cook for 10-12 minutes, until chicken is fully cooked.
5. Serve hot, garnished with fresh cilantro.

Mediterranean Lentil Soup

Ingredients:

- 1 tablespoon olive oil
- 1 onion, chopped
- 2 carrots, chopped
- 2 celery stalks, chopped
- 2 garlic cloves, minced
- 1 can (14 oz) diced tomatoes
- 1 1/2 cups dried lentils, rinsed
- 4 cups vegetable broth
- 1 teaspoon cumin
- 1 teaspoon coriander
- 1 bay leaf
- 2 tablespoons fresh parsley, chopped
- Salt and pepper to taste

Instructions:

1. Heat olive oil in a large pot over medium heat. Add onion, carrots, celery, and garlic, cooking until softened.
2. Stir in the tomatoes, lentils, vegetable broth, cumin, coriander, and bay leaf.
3. Bring to a boil, then reduce to a simmer and cook for 25-30 minutes until the lentils are tender.
4. Season with salt and pepper.
5. Serve hot, garnished with fresh parsley.

Chinese Hot and Sour Soup

Ingredients:

- 4 cups chicken or vegetable broth
- 1/2 cup sliced mushrooms
- 1/2 cup bamboo shoots, sliced
- 1/2 cup tofu, cubed
- 2 tablespoons soy sauce
- 2 tablespoons rice vinegar
- 1 tablespoon sesame oil
- 1 teaspoon chili paste
- 1 tablespoon cornstarch mixed with 1 tablespoon water
- 1 egg, beaten
- Fresh cilantro for garnish

Instructions:

1. In a pot, bring the broth to a boil.
2. Add mushrooms, bamboo shoots, tofu, soy sauce, rice vinegar, sesame oil, and chili paste.
3. Simmer for 5 minutes.
4. Stir in the cornstarch mixture and cook for an additional 2-3 minutes to thicken.
5. Slowly pour the beaten egg into the soup while stirring to create egg ribbons.
6. Serve hot, garnished with fresh cilantro.

Moroccan Harira Soup

Ingredients:

- 2 tablespoons olive oil
- 1 onion, chopped
- 2 celery stalks, chopped
- 1 can (14 oz) diced tomatoes
- 1/2 cup lentils
- 1/4 cup chickpeas, drained
- 1 teaspoon ground cinnamon
- 1 teaspoon ground ginger
- 1 teaspoon turmeric
- 1/2 teaspoon cumin
- 4 cups vegetable or chicken broth
- 1/4 cup fresh parsley, chopped
- 1/4 cup fresh cilantro, chopped
- Lemon wedges for serving

Instructions:

1. Heat olive oil in a large pot over medium heat. Add onion and celery, cooking until softened.
2. Stir in tomatoes, lentils, chickpeas, and spices.
3. Add the broth, then bring to a boil and simmer for 30-40 minutes until the lentils are tender.
4. Stir in fresh parsley and cilantro, then season with salt and pepper.
5. Serve hot, garnished with lemon wedges.

Korean Kimchi Stew (Kimchi Jjigae)

Ingredients:

- 2 cups kimchi, chopped
- 1 tablespoon sesame oil
- 1 onion, sliced
- 2 garlic cloves, minced
- 2 cups pork belly or tofu, cubed
- 4 cups chicken or vegetable broth
- 2 teaspoons gochujang (Korean chili paste)
- 1 tablespoon soy sauce
- 2 green onions, chopped

Instructions:

1. Heat sesame oil in a pot over medium heat. Add onion and garlic, cooking until softened.
2. Stir in pork belly or tofu and cook until browned.
3. Add kimchi, gochujang, soy sauce, and broth, then bring to a simmer.
4. Simmer for 20-30 minutes to allow the flavors to meld.
5. Serve hot, garnished with green onions.

Italian Minestrone

Ingredients:

- 1 tablespoon olive oil
- 1 onion, chopped
- 2 carrots, chopped
- 2 celery stalks, chopped
- 2 garlic cloves, minced
- 1 zucchini, chopped
- 1 potato, peeled and diced
- 1 can (14 oz) diced tomatoes
- 4 cups vegetable or chicken broth
- 1 can (14 oz) cannellini beans, drained and rinsed
- 1 cup pasta (small shapes like elbow or ditalini)
- 1 teaspoon dried oregano
- Salt and pepper to taste
- Fresh basil for garnish
- Parmesan cheese for serving

Instructions:

1. Heat olive oil in a large pot over medium heat. Add onion, carrots, celery, and garlic, and sauté until softened.
2. Stir in zucchini, potato, diced tomatoes, vegetable broth, and cannellini beans. Bring to a boil.
3. Add the pasta, oregano, salt, and pepper. Reduce heat to a simmer and cook for 10-12 minutes until the pasta is tender.
4. Adjust seasoning with salt and pepper.
5. Serve hot, garnished with fresh basil and a sprinkle of Parmesan cheese.

Caribbean Goat Curry

Ingredients:

- 2 lbs goat meat, cut into chunks
- 2 tablespoons curry powder
- 1 tablespoon allspice
- 2 cloves garlic, minced
- 1 onion, chopped
- 1 scotch bonnet pepper, chopped (or substitute with mild pepper)
- 1 can (14 oz) coconut milk
- 4 cups beef or vegetable broth
- 2 potatoes, diced
- 2 carrots, chopped
- 1 teaspoon thyme
- 1 tablespoon brown sugar
- Salt and pepper to taste
- Fresh cilantro for garnish

Instructions:

1. In a large bowl, season the goat meat with curry powder, allspice, garlic, and salt. Let marinate for at least 1 hour.
2. In a large pot, heat some oil over medium heat. Brown the goat meat in batches, then remove and set aside.
3. In the same pot, sauté onions and scotch bonnet pepper until softened.
4. Return the goat meat to the pot, add the coconut milk, broth, thyme, and brown sugar. Bring to a boil, then reduce to a simmer.
5. Add the potatoes and carrots, and cook for 1-1.5 hours until the meat is tender.
6. Serve hot, garnished with fresh cilantro.

Ethiopian Misir Wat

Ingredients:

- 1 1/2 cups lentils (red or brown)
- 1 onion, chopped
- 3 garlic cloves, minced
- 1 tablespoon ginger, grated
- 1/4 cup berbere spice mix (or substitute with a mix of paprika, cumin, and chili powder)
- 1 can (14 oz) crushed tomatoes
- 3 cups vegetable broth
- 2 tablespoons niter kibbeh (Ethiopian spiced clarified butter) or regular butter
- Salt to taste
- Fresh cilantro for garnish

Instructions:

1. Rinse the lentils and set them aside.
2. In a large pot, heat the niter kibbeh or butter over medium heat. Add the onion and sauté until softened.
3. Add the garlic, ginger, and berbere spice mix. Stir for 1-2 minutes until fragrant.
4. Stir in the crushed tomatoes, vegetable broth, and lentils. Bring to a boil.
5. Lower the heat and simmer for 30-40 minutes, stirring occasionally, until the lentils are soft and the mixture thickens.
6. Season with salt to taste.
7. Serve hot, garnished with fresh cilantro.

Greek Avgolemono Soup

Ingredients:

- 6 cups chicken broth
- 1 cup orzo pasta
- 2 cups cooked chicken, shredded
- 3 eggs
- 1/4 cup lemon juice
- Salt and pepper to taste
- Fresh dill or parsley for garnish

Instructions:

1. In a large pot, bring the chicken broth to a boil. Add the orzo pasta and cook according to the package instructions.
2. Add the shredded chicken to the pot and reduce the heat to low.
3. In a separate bowl, whisk the eggs with the lemon juice.
4. Slowly ladle some hot broth into the egg mixture, whisking constantly to temper the eggs.
5. Slowly pour the egg mixture into the soup, stirring constantly until the soup thickens.
6. Season with salt and pepper.
7. Serve hot, garnished with fresh dill or parsley.

Spanish Gazpacho

Ingredients:

- 4 ripe tomatoes, chopped
- 1 cucumber, peeled and chopped
- 1 red bell pepper, chopped
- 1 small red onion, chopped
- 2 cloves garlic, minced
- 1/4 cup red wine vinegar
- 1/4 cup olive oil
- Salt and pepper to taste
- Fresh basil or parsley for garnish

Instructions:

1. In a blender or food processor, combine the tomatoes, cucumber, bell pepper, onion, garlic, vinegar, and olive oil. Blend until smooth.
2. Season with salt and pepper to taste.
3. Chill in the refrigerator for at least 1-2 hours before serving.
4. Serve cold, garnished with fresh basil or parsley.

Peruvian Chicken Soup (Aguadito de Pollo)

Ingredients:

- 1 lb chicken thighs, bone-in, skin removed
- 6 cups chicken broth
- 1/2 cup rice
- 1/2 cup cilantro leaves
- 1/2 cup green peas
- 1 carrot, chopped
- 2 cloves garlic, minced
- 1 onion, chopped
- 1 teaspoon cumin
- 1/2 teaspoon turmeric
- Salt and pepper to taste

Instructions:

1. In a large pot, bring the chicken broth to a boil. Add the chicken thighs and cook until tender, about 25 minutes.
2. Remove the chicken from the pot, discard the bones, and shred the meat.
3. Add rice, cilantro, peas, carrot, garlic, onion, cumin, turmeric, salt, and pepper to the pot. Simmer until the rice is cooked and the soup has thickened, about 20 minutes.
4. Return the shredded chicken to the soup and cook for an additional 5 minutes.
5. Serve hot.

Indonesian Soto Ayam

Ingredients:

- 1 lb chicken breast, bone-in
- 6 cups chicken broth
- 1 stalk lemongrass, smashed
- 3 cloves garlic, minced
- 2 teaspoons turmeric powder
- 2 teaspoons ginger, grated
- 1 teaspoon cumin
- 1 tablespoon soy sauce
- 2 boiled eggs, halved
- 1/4 cup fresh cilantro, chopped
- Bean sprouts for garnish
- Fried shallots for garnish
- 2 cups cooked rice

Instructions:

1. In a large pot, combine the chicken, broth, lemongrass, garlic, turmeric, ginger, cumin, and soy sauce. Bring to a boil and simmer for 30 minutes.
2. Remove the chicken, shred it, and return it to the pot.
3. To serve, place a spoonful of rice in each bowl and ladle the soup over it.
4. Top with boiled eggs, fresh cilantro, bean sprouts, and fried shallots.

Lebanese Fattoush Salad Bowl

Ingredients:

- 1 head Romaine lettuce, chopped
- 1 cucumber, chopped
- 1 tomato, chopped
- 1/4 cup red onion, thinly sliced
- 1/2 cup radishes, sliced
- 1/4 cup fresh parsley, chopped
- 1/4 cup fresh mint, chopped
- 2 tablespoons olive oil
- 1 tablespoon lemon juice
- 1 teaspoon pomegranate molasses
- 1/4 teaspoon sumac
- 2 pieces pita bread, toasted and broken into pieces
- Salt and pepper to taste

Instructions:

1. In a large bowl, combine the lettuce, cucumber, tomato, onion, radishes, parsley, and mint.
2. In a small bowl, whisk together the olive oil, lemon juice, pomegranate molasses, sumac, salt, and pepper.
3. Toss the dressing with the salad and top with the toasted pita pieces.
4. Serve immediately.

French Onion Soup

Ingredients:

- 4 large onions, thinly sliced
- 2 tablespoons butter
- 1 tablespoon olive oil
- 4 cups beef broth
- 1 cup dry white wine
- 1 tablespoon fresh thyme
- 1 bay leaf
- 1 teaspoon sugar
- 4 slices baguette, toasted
- 1 cup Gruyère cheese, grated

Instructions:

1. In a large pot, melt butter and olive oil over medium heat. Add onions and cook, stirring frequently, until they are caramelized, about 30 minutes.
2. Stir in the sugar and thyme, then add the wine and cook for 2-3 minutes.
3. Add the beef broth and bay leaf, bring to a boil, and simmer for 15 minutes.
4. Ladle the soup into bowls, place a slice of toasted baguette on top, and sprinkle with cheese.
5. Place under the broiler for 2-3 minutes until the cheese is melted and bubbly.
6. Serve hot.

Brazilian Feijoada Stew

Ingredients:

- 1 lb black beans, soaked overnight
- 1/2 lb pork shoulder, cut into chunks
- 1/2 lb smoked sausage, sliced
- 1/2 lb bacon, chopped
- 1 onion, chopped
- 3 cloves garlic, minced
- 2 bay leaves
- 1 teaspoon cumin
- Salt and pepper to taste
- 2 cups rice, cooked
- Fresh cilantro for garnish

Instructions:

1. In a large pot, sauté the bacon, sausage, and pork until browned.
2. Add the onion and garlic, cooking until softened.
3. Stir in the black beans, bay leaves, cumin, salt, and pepper, then add enough water to cover the beans.
4. Bring to a boil, then reduce the heat and simmer for 1.5-2 hours until the beans are tender.
5. Serve with rice and garnish with fresh cilantro.

Turkish Ezogelin Soup

Ingredients:

- 1 tablespoon olive oil
- 1 onion, chopped
- 2 cloves garlic, minced
- 1 carrot, grated
- 1/2 cup red lentils, rinsed
- 1/4 cup rice
- 1 tablespoon tomato paste
- 6 cups vegetable or chicken broth
- 1 teaspoon cumin
- 1/2 teaspoon paprika
- 1/2 teaspoon dried mint
- Salt and pepper to taste
- Fresh parsley for garnish
- Lemon wedges for serving

Instructions:

1. Heat olive oil in a large pot over medium heat. Add the onion and garlic, and sauté until softened.
2. Stir in the grated carrot, red lentils, and rice, and cook for 2-3 minutes.
3. Add tomato paste, vegetable broth, cumin, paprika, and mint. Bring to a boil.
4. Lower the heat and simmer for 30-40 minutes, until the lentils and rice are tender.
5. Season with salt and pepper.
6. Serve hot, garnished with fresh parsley and lemon wedges.

Israeli Shakshuka

Ingredients:

- 2 tablespoons olive oil
- 1 onion, chopped
- 1 bell pepper, chopped
- 3 garlic cloves, minced
- 1 can (14 oz) diced tomatoes
- 1 tablespoon tomato paste
- 1 teaspoon cumin
- 1 teaspoon paprika
- 1/2 teaspoon cayenne pepper
- Salt and pepper to taste
- 4-6 large eggs
- Fresh parsley for garnish
- Crusty bread for serving

Instructions:

1. Heat olive oil in a large skillet over medium heat. Add the onion and bell pepper, and sauté until softened.
2. Stir in garlic, diced tomatoes, tomato paste, cumin, paprika, cayenne, salt, and pepper. Simmer for 10-15 minutes until the sauce thickens.
3. Make small wells in the sauce and crack eggs into them. Cover the skillet and cook for 5-7 minutes, or until the eggs are cooked to your liking.
4. Garnish with fresh parsley.
5. Serve with crusty bread for dipping.

Thai Tom Yum Soup

Ingredients:

- 6 cups chicken or vegetable broth
- 2 stalks lemongrass, smashed
- 3-4 kaffir lime leaves, torn
- 3-4 Thai bird's eye chilies, smashed
- 2-3 slices galangal (or ginger)
- 1 cup mushrooms, sliced
- 1 cup cherry tomatoes, halved
- 1/2 cup fresh lime juice
- 2 tablespoons fish sauce
- 1 teaspoon sugar
- 1/2 cup fresh cilantro for garnish
- 1-2 shrimp or chicken breasts, cooked and chopped (optional)

Instructions:

1. In a large pot, bring the broth to a boil. Add lemongrass, lime leaves, chilies, and galangal. Simmer for 10-15 minutes to infuse the flavors.
2. Add the mushrooms and tomatoes, and cook for 5 minutes.
3. Stir in lime juice, fish sauce, and sugar. Adjust seasoning as needed.
4. Add shrimp or chicken if using, and cook for 2-3 more minutes.
5. Serve hot, garnished with fresh cilantro.

Mexican Pozole

Ingredients:

- 2 lbs pork shoulder or chicken, cut into chunks
- 1 can (15 oz) hominy, drained
- 6 cups chicken broth
- 2 cloves garlic, minced
- 1 onion, chopped
- 1 can (4 oz) diced green chilies
- 2 tablespoons chili powder
- 1 teaspoon cumin
- 1 teaspoon oregano
- Salt and pepper to taste
- Fresh cilantro, shredded cabbage, radishes, and lime wedges for garnish

Instructions:

1. In a large pot, combine the pork or chicken, hominy, chicken broth, garlic, onion, chilies, chili powder, cumin, and oregano. Bring to a boil.
2. Reduce the heat and simmer for 1-1.5 hours, until the meat is tender.
3. Remove the meat, shred it, and return it to the pot.
4. Season with salt and pepper to taste.
5. Serve hot, garnished with cilantro, cabbage, radishes, and lime wedges.

Russian Borscht

Ingredients:

- 2 tablespoons olive oil
- 1 onion, chopped
- 2 cloves garlic, minced
- 1 carrot, grated
- 1 beetroot, peeled and grated
- 1/2 small head cabbage, shredded
- 4 cups beef or vegetable broth
- 1 tablespoon tomato paste
- 2 tablespoons vinegar
- 1 teaspoon sugar
- Salt and pepper to taste
- 1/4 cup sour cream for serving
- Fresh dill for garnish

Instructions:

1. Heat olive oil in a large pot over medium heat. Add the onion and garlic, and sauté until softened.
2. Add the grated carrot and beetroot, and cook for another 5 minutes.
3. Stir in the cabbage, broth, tomato paste, vinegar, and sugar. Bring to a boil, then reduce heat and simmer for 40 minutes.
4. Season with salt and pepper.
5. Serve hot, topped with a dollop of sour cream and fresh dill.

Sri Lankan Dhal Curry

Ingredients:

- 1 cup red lentils, rinsed
- 1 onion, chopped
- 2 cloves garlic, minced
- 1 inch ginger, grated
- 1 green chili, chopped (optional)
- 1/2 teaspoon turmeric
- 1/2 teaspoon cumin
- 1/2 teaspoon mustard seeds
- 1/2 teaspoon coriander
- 1 can (14 oz) coconut milk
- 2 cups water
- Salt to taste
- Fresh cilantro for garnish

Instructions:

1. In a large pot, sauté the onion, garlic, ginger, and green chili in oil until softened.
2. Add the spices (turmeric, cumin, mustard seeds, coriander) and cook for 1-2 minutes until fragrant.
3. Stir in the lentils, coconut milk, and water. Bring to a boil, then reduce heat and simmer for 25-30 minutes, until the lentils are soft.
4. Season with salt.
5. Serve hot, garnished with fresh cilantro.

Jamaican Red Bean Soup

Ingredients:

- 1 cup dried red kidney beans, soaked overnight
- 4 cups water or broth
- 1 onion, chopped
- 2 cloves garlic, minced
- 1 carrot, chopped
- 1 stalk celery, chopped
- 1 Scotch bonnet pepper, chopped (optional)
- 1 teaspoon thyme
- 1 teaspoon allspice
- Salt and pepper to taste
- 1 tablespoon coconut milk (optional)
- Fresh cilantro for garnish

Instructions:

1. In a large pot, add the soaked beans, water or broth, onion, garlic, carrot, celery, Scotch bonnet pepper, thyme, and allspice. Bring to a boil.
2. Reduce heat and simmer for 1-1.5 hours until the beans are tender.
3. Season with salt and pepper.
4. Add coconut milk if desired and stir to combine.
5. Serve hot, garnished with fresh cilantro.

Chinese Wonton Soup

Ingredients:

- 1 pack of wonton wrappers
- 1/2 lb ground pork or shrimp
- 2 tablespoons soy sauce
- 1 tablespoon sesame oil
- 1 teaspoon grated ginger
- 1 clove garlic, minced
- 4 cups chicken broth
- 1 tablespoon soy sauce
- 1/2 teaspoon sugar
- 1/4 cup green onions, chopped
- Fresh cilantro for garnish

Instructions:

1. In a bowl, combine the ground pork or shrimp, soy sauce, sesame oil, ginger, and garlic. Mix until well combined.
2. Place a small spoonful of the filling in the center of each wonton wrapper. Wet the edges with water and fold to seal.
3. Bring the chicken broth to a boil in a large pot. Add the wontons and cook for 4-5 minutes, until they float to the surface.
4. Stir in soy sauce, sugar, and green onions.
5. Serve hot, garnished with cilantro.

Indian Sambar

Ingredients:

- 1 cup yellow split peas (toor dal), rinsed
- 1 onion, chopped
- 2 tomatoes, chopped
- 1 carrot, chopped
- 1/2 eggplant, chopped
- 2 tablespoons sambar powder
- 1 teaspoon turmeric
- 1 tablespoon tamarind paste
- 6 cups water or vegetable broth
- Salt to taste
- Fresh cilantro for garnish

Instructions:

1. In a large pot, cook the split peas in water or broth until soft, about 20-25 minutes.
2. Add the onion, tomatoes, carrot, eggplant, sambar powder, turmeric, and tamarind paste. Cook for another 15 minutes, until the vegetables are tender.
3. Season with salt to taste.
4. Serve hot, garnished with fresh cilantro.

Cambodian Amok Fish Stew

Ingredients:

- 1 lb white fish fillets (like tilapia or catfish), cut into chunks
- 1 tablespoon red curry paste
- 1 can (14 oz) coconut milk
- 2 tablespoons fish sauce
- 1 tablespoon brown sugar
- 1 cup bamboo shoots, sliced
- 1/2 cup fresh cilantro, chopped
- 2-3 kaffir lime leaves, torn
- 1 egg, beaten
- Salt to taste

Instructions:

1. In a large pot, combine the fish, curry paste, coconut milk, fish sauce, sugar, and bamboo shoots. Bring to a simmer.
2. Add the kaffir lime leaves and cook for 10 minutes.
3. Stir in the egg and cook for an additional 5 minutes until the stew thickens.
4. Season with salt to taste.
5. Serve hot, garnished with fresh cilantro.

Nigerian Egusi Soup

Ingredients:

- 1 cup ground egusi seeds (melon seeds)
- 1/2 lb beef or goat meat, cubed
- 1/2 lb smoked fish or stockfish, soaked and shredded
- 1/2 cup palm oil
- 1 onion, chopped
- 2 tomatoes, chopped
- 1-2 tablespoons ground crayfish
- 2 cups spinach or bitterleaf (washed)
- 1 tablespoon ground pepper (adjust to taste)
- 6 cups beef broth or water
- Salt to taste

Instructions:

1. In a large pot, cook the beef or goat meat with some salt and a little water until tender. Set aside.
2. In another pot, heat the palm oil over medium heat and add the onions, cooking until translucent.
3. Add the tomatoes, and cook for 10 minutes until softened.
4. Stir in the ground egusi seeds and cook, stirring frequently, for about 5 minutes.
5. Add the beef broth or water and bring the mixture to a boil.
6. Add the cooked meat, smoked fish, crayfish, ground pepper, and spinach or bitterleaf. Cook for 15-20 minutes until the soup thickens.
7. Season with salt to taste.
8. Serve hot with pounded yam, fufu, or rice.

Egyptian Molokhia

Ingredients:

- 1 lb molokhia (jute leaves), chopped (can substitute with frozen molokhia)
- 6 cups chicken broth
- 1 whole chicken, cut into pieces
- 4 cloves garlic, minced
- 2 tablespoons butter
- 1 teaspoon ground coriander
- 1/2 teaspoon ground cumin
- 1/2 teaspoon turmeric (optional)
- Salt and pepper to taste
- Lemon wedges for serving

Instructions:

1. In a large pot, cook the chicken in the chicken broth until tender, about 30 minutes. Remove the chicken, shred the meat, and set aside.
2. In a separate pan, melt butter and sauté garlic until fragrant. Add coriander, cumin, and turmeric, cooking for another minute.
3. Add the molokhia leaves to the garlic mixture and cook for 5-7 minutes.
4. Pour the cooked molokhia into the chicken broth and bring to a simmer.
5. Add the shredded chicken and cook for another 10-15 minutes.
6. Season with salt and pepper.
7. Serve hot, with lemon wedges on the side.

Italian Pappa al Pomodoro

Ingredients:

- 1 lb ripe tomatoes, chopped
- 1 small onion, chopped
- 3 cloves garlic, minced
- 1/4 cup extra virgin olive oil
- 2 cups vegetable broth
- 4 cups stale bread, cubed
- 1/4 cup fresh basil, chopped
- Salt and pepper to taste

Instructions:

1. In a large pot, heat olive oil over medium heat. Add the onion and garlic, and sauté until soft and fragrant.
2. Add the chopped tomatoes, vegetable broth, salt, and pepper, and bring to a simmer. Cook for 20 minutes, stirring occasionally.
3. Add the stale bread cubes, and cook for an additional 10-15 minutes, stirring until the bread breaks down and the soup thickens.
4. Stir in fresh basil and adjust seasoning as needed.
5. Serve hot, drizzled with extra olive oil and garnished with basil leaves.

Afghan Ashak

Ingredients:

- 2 cups all-purpose flour
- 1/2 teaspoon salt
- 1/4 teaspoon turmeric
- Water (as needed to form dough)
- 1 lb ground lamb or beef
- 1 onion, finely chopped
- 2 cloves garlic, minced
- 1 teaspoon ground coriander
- 1 teaspoon ground cumin
- 1/2 teaspoon ground turmeric
- 1/2 teaspoon cinnamon
- 1 cup yogurt
- Fresh cilantro for garnish

Instructions:

1. In a mixing bowl, combine flour, salt, and turmeric. Gradually add water and knead to form a soft dough. Let it rest for 20 minutes.
2. For the filling, sauté the onion and garlic until soft. Add the ground lamb or beef and cook until browned. Stir in coriander, cumin, turmeric, and cinnamon. Set aside to cool.
3. Roll out the dough and cut into small rounds. Place a spoonful of the meat filling in the center of each round and fold the dough into a dumpling shape.
4. Boil the dumplings in salted water for 10-12 minutes until they float to the surface.
5. Serve the dumplings with yogurt and fresh cilantro on top.

Malaysian Laksa

Ingredients:

- 2 tablespoons vegetable oil
- 1 onion, chopped
- 2 cloves garlic, minced
- 1-inch piece of ginger, minced
- 1 tablespoon red curry paste
- 1 can (14 oz) coconut milk
- 4 cups chicken broth
- 8 oz rice noodles, cooked
- 1 lb cooked shrimp, peeled
- 2 eggs, soft-boiled
- 1/4 cup bean sprouts
- 2-3 sprigs fresh cilantro, chopped
- Lime wedges for serving
- 1-2 tablespoons fish sauce

Instructions:

1. Heat the oil in a pot over medium heat. Add onion, garlic, and ginger, and cook until fragrant.
2. Stir in red curry paste and cook for another 2 minutes.
3. Add coconut milk, chicken broth, and fish sauce, and bring to a simmer.
4. Add the cooked rice noodles and shrimp, and cook for 5 minutes until heated through.
5. Serve the laksa in bowls, topped with soft-boiled eggs, bean sprouts, cilantro, and lime wedges.

Vietnamese Bun Bo Hue

Ingredients:

- 1 lb beef shank, cut into chunks
- 1/2 lb pork belly, sliced
- 8 cups water
- 1 onion, halved
- 2 lemongrass stalks, smashed
- 3-4 kaffir lime leaves
- 1 tablespoon shrimp paste
- 2 tablespoons chili oil
- 2 tablespoons fish sauce
- 1 tablespoon sugar
- 12 oz rice noodles
- Fresh herbs (mint, cilantro), lime wedges, and chili slices for garnish

Instructions:

1. In a large pot, combine beef shank, pork belly, and water. Bring to a boil, then reduce the heat and simmer for 1.5 hours.
2. Add the onion, lemongrass, kaffir lime leaves, shrimp paste, chili oil, fish sauce, and sugar. Simmer for another 30 minutes.
3. Remove the meat, shred it, and set aside.
4. Cook the rice noodles according to package instructions.
5. To serve, divide noodles into bowls, pour the broth over, and top with shredded meat, fresh herbs, lime wedges, and chili slices.

Filipino Sinigang na Baboy

Ingredients:

- 2 lbs pork (ribs or belly), cut into chunks
- 10 cups water
- 1 onion, quartered
- 2 tomatoes, quartered
- 2 long green chilies
- 1 packet sinigang mix (or 2 tablespoons tamarind paste)
- 1/2 daikon radish, sliced
- 1 eggplant, sliced
- 1 cup string beans
- 1 bunch kangkong (water spinach) or bok choy
- Fish sauce and salt to taste

Instructions:

1. In a large pot, bring water, pork, onion, tomatoes, and green chilies to a boil.
2. Reduce the heat and simmer for 1-1.5 hours until the pork is tender.
3. Add the sinigang mix or tamarind paste, daikon radish, eggplant, and string beans. Cook for 10 minutes.
4. Add the kangkong or bok choy and cook for an additional 2-3 minutes.
5. Season with fish sauce and salt to taste.
6. Serve hot with steamed rice.

Pakistani Haleem

Ingredients:

- 1/2 cup wheat (cracked or whole)
- 1/2 cup yellow split peas (chana dal)
- 1/2 cup lentils (moong dal)
- 1/2 lb boneless chicken or beef, cut into pieces
- 2 onions, thinly sliced
- 2 cloves garlic, minced
- 1-inch piece of ginger, minced
- 1 tablespoon ground coriander
- 1 tablespoon ground cumin
- 1 teaspoon ground turmeric
- 1 teaspoon garam masala
- 4 cups chicken or beef broth
- Fresh cilantro and fried onions for garnish
- Lemon wedges for serving

Instructions:

1. In a pot, cook the cracked wheat and lentils until soft. Set aside.
2. In a separate pot, sauté onions, garlic, and ginger until golden. Add the chicken or beef and cook until browned.
3. Add the spices (coriander, cumin, turmeric, garam masala) and cook for 5 minutes.
4. Add the cooked wheat and lentils, and broth. Simmer for 1 hour, stirring occasionally.
5. Once the meat is tender, blend the soup until smooth or leave it chunky, based on preference.
6. Garnish with fresh cilantro and fried onions, and serve with lemon wedges.

Tunisian Brik

Ingredients:

- 8 brik pastry sheets (or phyllo dough)
- 8 eggs
- 1/2 cup tuna, drained and flaked
- 1/4 cup capers
- 2 tablespoons parsley, chopped
- 1 tablespoon harissa (Tunisian chili paste)
- Olive oil for frying
- Salt and pepper to taste

Instructions:

1. Lay out one brik pastry sheet and place a spoonful of tuna, capers, parsley, and harissa in the center.
2. Gently crack an egg on top of the filling.
3. Fold the pastry over to form a triangle. Seal the edges tightly.
4. Heat olive oil in a frying pan over medium heat. Fry the brik for 2-3 minutes per side, until golden and crispy.
5. Serve hot, with additional harissa on the side.

Persian Fesenjan

Ingredients:

- 1 lb chicken thighs or duck, bone-in, skinless
- 1 large onion, finely chopped
- 1/2 cup pomegranate molasses
- 1 cup walnuts, finely ground
- 2 tablespoons vegetable oil
- 1 teaspoon ground turmeric
- 1 teaspoon ground cinnamon
- 1/2 teaspoon ground cumin
- 1/4 teaspoon ground ginger
- 2 cups chicken broth
- 1/2 cup sugar (optional, adjust to taste)
- Salt and pepper to taste
- Fresh pomegranate seeds for garnish
- Rice for serving

Instructions:

1. Heat the oil in a large pot over medium heat. Brown the chicken thighs or duck on all sides. Remove and set aside.
2. In the same pot, add the chopped onion and cook until golden and soft, about 5 minutes.
3. Stir in the turmeric, cinnamon, cumin, and ginger, and cook for another 1-2 minutes until fragrant.
4. Add the ground walnuts and cook for 3-4 minutes, stirring occasionally.
5. Pour in the chicken broth and pomegranate molasses, and bring to a boil.
6. Reduce the heat and return the chicken to the pot. Simmer uncovered for 45 minutes to 1 hour, until the sauce thickens and the chicken is tender.
7. Stir in the sugar (if desired) and adjust seasoning with salt and pepper.
8. Serve the Fesenjan over rice, garnished with fresh pomegranate seeds.

Greek Beef and Tomato Stew (Stifado)

Ingredients:

- 2 lbs beef stew meat, cubed
- 2 onions, chopped
- 4 cloves garlic, minced
- 2 tablespoons olive oil
- 2 cups canned tomatoes, crushed
- 1/2 cup red wine
- 1/4 cup red wine vinegar
- 1 cinnamon stick
- 2-3 whole cloves
- 1 teaspoon dried oregano
- 1 teaspoon ground allspice
- Salt and pepper to taste
- Fresh parsley for garnish
- Rice or crusty bread for serving

Instructions:

1. Heat the olive oil in a large pot over medium-high heat. Brown the beef cubes on all sides, then remove from the pot and set aside.
2. In the same pot, sauté the onions and garlic until soft, about 5 minutes.
3. Add the red wine, red wine vinegar, and crushed tomatoes. Stir in the cinnamon stick, cloves, oregano, and allspice.
4. Return the beef to the pot and add enough water to cover the meat. Bring to a boil.
5. Reduce the heat, cover, and simmer for 1.5 to 2 hours until the beef is tender and the sauce thickens.
6. Season with salt and pepper to taste.
7. Serve the stifado with rice or crusty bread, and garnish with fresh parsley.

South African Bunny Chow

Ingredients:

- 2 tablespoons vegetable oil
- 1 lb chicken thighs or lamb, cubed
- 1 large onion, chopped
- 3 cloves garlic, minced
- 1 tablespoon curry powder
- 1 teaspoon ground turmeric
- 1 teaspoon ground cumin
- 1/2 teaspoon ground coriander
- 2 tomatoes, chopped
- 1 cup coconut milk
- 1/2 cup vegetable broth
- 2 cups cubed white bread (preferably unsliced loaf bread)
- Fresh cilantro for garnish
- Salt and pepper to taste

Instructions:

1. Heat the vegetable oil in a large pot over medium heat. Add the chicken or lamb cubes and cook until browned.
2. Add the chopped onion and garlic, cooking until softened, about 5 minutes.
3. Stir in the curry powder, turmeric, cumin, and coriander, and cook for 1-2 minutes until fragrant.
4. Add the chopped tomatoes, coconut milk, and vegetable broth, and bring the mixture to a simmer.
5. Reduce the heat and cook for 30 minutes, until the meat is tender and the sauce thickens.
6. Season with salt and pepper to taste.
7. To serve, hollow out the center of a loaf of white bread, leaving a shell.
8. Fill the bread with the curry mixture and garnish with fresh cilantro.

Japanese Miso Soup

Ingredients:

- 4 cups dashi (Japanese fish stock)
- 3 tablespoons white or red miso paste
- 1/2 block silken tofu, cut into small cubes
- 1/4 cup chopped green onions
- 1 tablespoon dried wakame seaweed
- Soy sauce (optional, for seasoning)

Instructions:

1. In a pot, bring the dashi to a simmer over medium heat.
2. Whisk in the miso paste until fully dissolved, adjusting the amount to taste (more for stronger flavor).
3. Add the tofu cubes and dried wakame seaweed to the pot, and cook for 2-3 minutes until the tofu is heated through.
4. Stir in the chopped green onions.
5. Taste the soup, and if desired, add a splash of soy sauce for extra seasoning.
6. Serve the soup hot, garnished with additional green onions if desired.

Filipino Adobo

Ingredients:

- 2 lbs chicken or pork (or a mix), cut into pieces
- 1 onion, sliced
- 6 cloves garlic, minced
- 1/2 cup soy sauce
- 1/4 cup vinegar
- 1 tablespoon brown sugar
- 2 bay leaves
- 1/2 teaspoon black peppercorns
- 1/2 cup water
- 1 tablespoon vegetable oil
- Steamed rice for serving

Instructions:

1. In a bowl, combine the chicken or pork with soy sauce, vinegar, minced garlic, bay leaves, and peppercorns. Marinate for at least 30 minutes (or overnight in the fridge).
2. Heat vegetable oil in a large pot over medium heat. Add the marinated meat and cook until browned on all sides.
3. Pour in the marinade, add the water, and stir in the brown sugar. Bring to a boil.
4. Lower the heat and simmer for 45 minutes to 1 hour, or until the meat is tender and the sauce has reduced.
5. Taste and adjust seasoning with salt or additional soy sauce if needed.
6. Serve hot with steamed rice.

Hawaiian Poke Bowl

Ingredients:

- 1 lb sushi-grade tuna or salmon, cubed
- 2 tablespoons soy sauce
- 1 tablespoon sesame oil
- 1 teaspoon rice vinegar
- 1 teaspoon honey
- 1/4 teaspoon chili flakes (optional)
- 1/2 avocado, sliced
- 1/2 cucumber, thinly sliced
- 1/4 cup shredded carrots
- 1/4 cup edamame beans (cooked)
- 1/4 cup seaweed salad
- 1 tablespoon sesame seeds
- 1 tablespoon green onions, chopped
- 2 cups cooked white rice (preferably sushi rice)

Instructions:

1. In a bowl, combine the soy sauce, sesame oil, rice vinegar, honey, and chili flakes (if using). Stir well to combine.
2. Add the cubed tuna or salmon to the marinade and toss gently to coat. Let marinate for 10-15 minutes in the fridge.
3. To assemble the poke bowl, divide the rice between two bowls.
4. Arrange the marinated fish, avocado, cucumber, shredded carrots, edamame, and seaweed salad on top of the rice.
5. Sprinkle with sesame seeds and chopped green onions.
6. Serve immediately and enjoy!

South Korean Bibimbap

Ingredients:

- 1 cup cooked white rice
- 1/2 lb ground beef (or chicken)
- 1 tablespoon soy sauce
- 1 tablespoon sesame oil
- 1 teaspoon sugar
- 1 teaspoon minced garlic
- 1/4 teaspoon ground black pepper
- 1/2 cup spinach, blanched and squeezed dry
- 1/2 cup bean sprouts, blanched
- 1/2 carrot, julienned
- 1 egg (fried sunny-side up)
- 2 tablespoons gochujang (Korean chili paste)
- 1 tablespoon sesame seeds
- 1 tablespoon green onions, chopped

Instructions:

1. Cook the rice and set aside.
2. In a pan, cook the ground beef with soy sauce, sesame oil, sugar, garlic, and pepper. Stir-fry until browned and cooked through.
3. Blanch the spinach and bean sprouts, then squeeze out excess water. Season both with a little sesame oil and salt.
4. In a separate pan, sauté the julienned carrots until slightly tender.
5. To assemble the bibimbap, place the cooked rice in a large bowl. Arrange the cooked beef, spinach, bean sprouts, carrots, and egg on top of the rice.
6. Add a spoonful of gochujang in the center, and sprinkle with sesame seeds and green onions.
7. Serve and mix everything together before eating.

Cuban Ropa Vieja

Ingredients:

- 2 lbs flank steak or skirt steak
- 1 tablespoon olive oil
- 1 onion, sliced
- 1 bell pepper, sliced
- 4 cloves garlic, minced
- 1 (14 oz) can diced tomatoes
- 1/4 cup dry white wine
- 1/4 cup green olives, chopped
- 1/4 cup capers
- 1 tablespoon tomato paste
- 1 teaspoon cumin
- 1 teaspoon paprika
- 1/2 teaspoon oregano
- 1/2 teaspoon bay leaf
- Salt and pepper to taste
- Cooked rice for serving

Instructions:

1. In a large pot, heat olive oil over medium-high heat. Sear the flank steak until browned on both sides, then remove and set aside.
2. In the same pot, add the onions, bell pepper, and garlic. Sauté until softened, about 5 minutes.
3. Add the diced tomatoes, white wine, olives, capers, tomato paste, cumin, paprika, oregano, and bay leaf. Stir well.
4. Return the steak to the pot and add enough water to cover the meat. Bring to a boil, then reduce to a simmer.
5. Cover and cook for 2-3 hours, or until the meat is tender and shreds easily.
6. Once the beef is cooked, shred it with two forks. Stir the shredded beef into the sauce.
7. Serve over rice.

Israeli Sabich Bowl

Ingredients:

- 1 medium eggplant, sliced
- 2 tablespoons olive oil
- 1/4 teaspoon ground cumin
- 1/4 teaspoon ground coriander
- Salt and pepper to taste
- 2 hard-boiled eggs, sliced
- 1 cup hummus
- 1/2 cup Israeli salad (tomatoes, cucumber, red onion, parsley)
- 1 tablespoon tahini
- 1 tablespoon lemon juice
- Pita bread for serving

Instructions:

1. Preheat the oven to 400°F (200°C).
2. Toss the eggplant slices with olive oil, cumin, coriander, salt, and pepper. Arrange on a baking sheet and roast for 20-25 minutes until tender and golden.
3. In a small bowl, mix the tahini and lemon juice, adding a little water to thin it out if needed.
4. To assemble the sabich bowls, spread hummus at the bottom of each bowl. Top with roasted eggplant, hard-boiled eggs, and Israeli salad.
5. Drizzle with tahini sauce and serve with pita bread on the side.

Moroccan Chickpea and Tomato Soup

Ingredients:

- 1 tablespoon olive oil
- 1 onion, chopped
- 2 cloves garlic, minced
- 1 teaspoon ground cumin
- 1 teaspoon ground turmeric
- 1 teaspoon ground cinnamon
- 1 (14 oz) can chickpeas, drained and rinsed
- 1 (14 oz) can diced tomatoes
- 4 cups vegetable broth
- Salt and pepper to taste
- Fresh cilantro for garnish
- Lemon wedges for serving

Instructions:

1. In a large pot, heat olive oil over medium heat. Add the onion and garlic, and sauté until softened.
2. Stir in the cumin, turmeric, and cinnamon, cooking for 1 minute until fragrant.
3. Add the chickpeas, tomatoes, and vegetable broth. Bring to a boil, then reduce the heat and simmer for 20 minutes.
4. Season with salt and pepper to taste.
5. Serve the soup hot, garnished with fresh cilantro and lemon wedges.

New Zealand Kumara Soup

Ingredients:

- 2 medium kumara (sweet potatoes), peeled and diced
- 1 onion, chopped
- 2 cloves garlic, minced
- 1 tablespoon olive oil
- 4 cups vegetable broth
- 1/2 teaspoon ground ginger
- Salt and pepper to taste
- Fresh cream or coconut milk for serving

Instructions:

1. Heat the olive oil in a large pot over medium heat. Add the onion and garlic, and sauté until softened.
2. Add the diced kumara and cook for 5 minutes, stirring occasionally.
3. Pour in the vegetable broth and bring to a boil. Reduce the heat and simmer for 20-25 minutes, until the kumara is tender.
4. Use an immersion blender or regular blender to puree the soup until smooth.
5. Season with salt and pepper.
6. Serve with a swirl of fresh cream or coconut milk.

Indonesian Gado-Gado

Ingredients:

- 2 cups steamed rice
- 1/2 head napa cabbage, shredded
- 1 cup bean sprouts
- 1 cucumber, sliced
- 2 hard-boiled eggs, sliced
- 1/4 cup roasted peanuts, crushed
- 1/4 cup fried shallots
- 1/4 cup sambal oelek (optional for heat)
- 1/4 cup peanut butter
- 2 tablespoons soy sauce
- 1 tablespoon brown sugar
- 1 tablespoon lime juice
- 1/4 cup warm water

Instructions:

1. Arrange the steamed rice, napa cabbage, bean sprouts, cucumber, and hard-boiled eggs in individual bowls.
2. In a small bowl, mix together the sambal oelek (if using), peanut butter, soy sauce, brown sugar, lime juice, and warm water to create the sauce.
3. Drizzle the sauce over the vegetables and rice.
4. Sprinkle with crushed peanuts and fried shallots for garnish.
5. Serve immediately.